T0071126

Songs and Cries of London Town

Bob Chilcott

a 'capital' choral cantata for SATB choir, upper-voice choir, piano duet, and optional percussion

1. Come buy (anon.) 1
2. The flower of Cities all (William Dunbar) 16
3. London bells (anon.) 21
4. Composed upon Westminster Bridge, September 3, 1802 (William Wordsworth) 33
5. Good morrow! (anon.) 40

MUSIC DEPARTMENT

OXFORD
UNIVERSITY PRESS

OXFORD
UNIVERSITY PRESS

Great Clarendon Street, Oxford OX2 6DP, England
198 Madison Avenue, New York, NY10016, USA

Oxford University Press is a department of the University of Oxford.
It furthers the University's aim of excellence in research, scholarship,
and education by publishing worldwide in

Oxford New York
Auckland Bangkok Buenos Aires Cape Town Chennai
Dar es Salaam Delhi Hong Kong Istanbul Karachi Kolkata
Kuala Lumpur Madrid Melbourne Mexico City Mumbai Nairobi
São Paulo Shanghai Taipei Tokyo Toronto

Oxford is a registered trade mark of Oxford University Press
in the UK and in certain other countries

© Oxford University Press 2001

The moral rights of the author have been asserted

Database right Oxford University Press (maker)

First published 2001

All rights reserved. No part of this publication may be reproduced,
stored in a retrieval system, or transmitted, in any form or by any means,
without the prior permission in writing of Oxford University Press,
or as expressly permitted by law. Enquiries concerning reproduction
outside the scope of the above should be sent to the Music Copyright
Department, Oxford University Press, at the address above

Permission to perform this work in public
(except in the course of divine worship) should normally be obtained
from the Performing Right Society Ltd. (PRS), 29/33 Berners Street,
London W1T 3AB, or its affiliated Societies in each country throughout
the world, unless the owner or the occupier of the premises
being used holds a licence from the Society

Permission to make a recording must be obtained in advance
from the Mechanical Copyright Protection Society Ltd. (MCPS),
Elgar House, 41 Streatham High Road, London SW16 1ER,
or its affiliated Societies in each country throughout the world

ISBN 978-0-19-343297-0

Printed in Great Britain on acid-free paper by
Halstan & Co. Ltd., Amersham, Bucks.

London bells (No. 3), with accompaniment arranged for one piano, is also available as a stand-alone piece in a separate leaflet alongside the upper-voice part for *Good morrow!* (No. 5). The leaflet (BC47a, ISBN 0-19-343333-8) may be used in conjunction with this vocal score.

Commissioned by and dedicated to Colin Durrant and the Barnet Choral Society, on the occasion of the choir's Diamond Jubilee

Songs and Cries of London Town

1. *Come buy*

Anon (17th century)

BOB CHILCOTT

© Oxford University Press 2001

Printed in Great Britain

OXFORD UNIVERSITY PRESS, MUSIC DEPARTMENT, GREAT CLARENDON STREET, OXFORD OX2 6DP

Photocopying this copyright material is ILLEGAL.

8
- vy.
Here's fe - ther - few,
gil - li-flowers and rue.
11
ff
mp
Come buy my knot-ted mar-jo - rum, HO!
Come buy my mint, my
mp leggiero
mp
mp leggiero
mp
Triangle
mp

15
cresc.
fine green mint. Here's fine la-ven-der for your cloaths. Here's pars-ley and
cresc.
cresc.
cresc.
19
mf legato
win - ter - sa-vo-ry, And hearts-ease, which all do choose.
mf
mp leggiero
mf

23
mp
mf cresc.
Here's balm and his-sop, and cinque - foil, All fine herbs, it is well known.
mp
mf
mp
mf
mp
27
f
Let none des-pise the mer - ry, mer-ry cries of
TENORS & BASSES f
Let none des - pise the mer - ry, mer - ry
f
f
Bongos
mf
f

30
gliss.
f
fa - mous Lon - don town!
Let none des - pise the
gliss.
f
cries of fa - mous Lon - don town!
Let none des -
33
ff
mer - ry, mer - ry cries of fa - mous Lon - don town! HO!
ff
- pise the mer - ry cries of fa - mous Lon - don town! HO!
ff
f
ff
f
ff
f

37
TENORS & BASSES
f
Here's fine her-rings,
41
eight a groat.
Hot cod - lins, pies and tarts.
New mack - erel!

45
ff
have to sell.
Come buy my Well - fleet oys - ters, HO!
mp leggiero
mp leggiero
mp
49
cresc.
Come buy my whit - ings fine and new.
Wives, shall I mend your hus - bands' horns? I'll
mp
mp
Triangle
mp

53
mf espress.
grind your knives to please your wives,
And ve - ry nice - ly cut your
cresc.
mf
cresc.
mf
cresc.

57
mp
mf cresc.
corns.
Maids, have you a - ny hair to sell,
Ei - ther flax - en,
mp leggiero
mp
mf
mp
mf
mp

61
SOPRANOS & ALTOS
f
Let none des-pise the mer-ry, mer-ry cries of
black or brown?
Let none des - pise the mer-ry, mer-ry
Bongos
mf
65
gliss.
fa - mous Lon - don town!
Let none des-pise the mer-ry, mer-ry cries of
cries of fa - mous Lon - don town!
Let none des - pise the mer-ry cries of

69
ff
fa - mous Lon - don town! HO!
ff
fa - mous Lon - don town! HO!
ff
f
ff
f
ff
f
73
f
Here's fine_ ros-ma - ry, sage, and_ thyme.
f
Here's fine her-rings, eight a groat.

77
Come buy my ground i - vy.
Here's fe-ther-few,
Hot cod - lins, pies and tarts.
New mack - erel!
80
gil - li-flowers and rue.
Come buy my knot-ted mar-jo - rum, HO!
ff
have to sell.
Come buy my Well - fleet oys - ters, HO!
ff
mp leggiero

83
mp
Come buy my mint, my fine green mint. Here's fine la-ven-der
mp
Come buy my whit-ings fine and new. Wives, shall I mend your
mp
mp leggiero
mp
Triangle
mp
87
cresc.
mf legato
for your cloaths. Here's pars-ley and win-ter-sa-vo-ry, And hearts-ease, which
cresc.
mf espress.
hus-bands' horns? I'll grind your knives to please your wives, And ve-ry
cresc.
mf
cresc.
mf
cresc.

91
mp
mf cresc.
all do choose.
Here's balm and his-sop, and cinque-foil,
All fine herbs, it
nice-ly cut your corns.
Maids, have you a - ny hair to sell,
Ei-ther flax-en,
mp leggiero
mp
mf
96
f
is well known.
Let none des-pise the mer-ry, mer-ry cries of
black or brown?
Let none des-pise the mer-ry, mer-ry
Bongos
mf

100
gliss.
f
fa - mous Lon - don town!
Let none des-pise the mer-ry, mer-ry cries of
cries of fa - mous Lon - don town!
Let none des - pise the mer-ry cries of
104
ff
fa - mous Lon - don town!
Let none des-pise the mer-ry, mer-ry cries of
fa - mous Lon - don town!

108
gliss.
ff
fa - mous Lon - don town!
Let none des-pise the
111
fff
mer-ry, mer-ry cries Of fa - mous Lon - don town!
HO!
attacca

2. *The flower of Cities all*

William Dunbar (1465?–1530?)

123
poco rit.
a tempo
dolce
p
wal - lès run-neth down;
dolce
p
poco rit.
a tempo
p
6
p sost.
6
6
p dolce
128
SOPRANOS
p legato
Where many a swan doth swim with
6
3
3
3
3
3
3
3
3
p legato
3
3
p
3
3

131
mp espress.
win - gès fair, Where many a barge doth sail, and row with oar,
ALTOS
Where
p
p
134
S.
A.
T.
B.
cresc.
f appass.
many a ship doth rest with top - roy - al.
O
f appass.
mp cantabile
cresc.

137
town of town - ès, pa - tron and not com - pare,
f
f
Large suspended cymbal
tr
mf
ff molto dim.
140
Lon - don,
ff molto dim.
ff molto dim.
p dolce
ff molto dim.
mp
p
ff

143
poco rit.
a tempo
p dolce
mp espress.
S.
thou_ art
the flower of Ci - - ties all,
A.
thou_ art the flower of Ci - ties all,
of Ci - ties all, the
T.
thou_ art
the flower, the flower of
B.
thou_ art
the flower of___ Ci - - ties all,
poco rit.
a tempo
mp
146
p
pp
the flower of Ci - ties all,
the flower of
flower of Ci - ties all,
of Ci - ties all,
the flower of Ci - ties all,
of
Ci - ties all,
the flower,
the flower of Ci - ties all,
of
the flower of___ Ci - ties all,
the flower of___

3. *London bells*

Anon. (early 18th century)

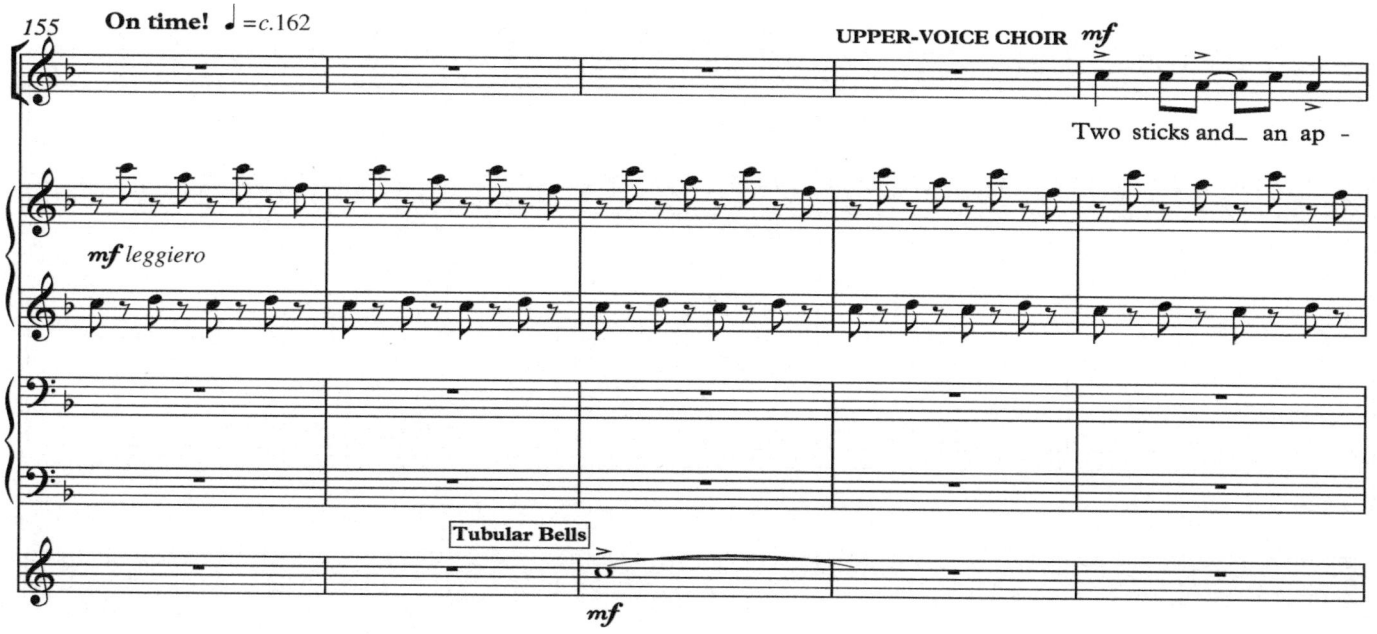

160
-ple, Ring the bells at White - cha - pel.

165
Old Fa - ther Bald Pate, Ring the bells Ald - gate.

170
Maids in white a - prons,
175
Ring the bells at St Cath - erine's.

180
O - ran - ges and le - mons, Ring the bells at St Cle - ment's.
184
f
When will you pay me?
f
f

189
Ring the bells at the Old Bai - ley. When I am rich, Ring the bells at Fleet-
194
-ditch.
When will that
f
f
f

199
be? Ring the bells at Step - ney. When I am
f cresc.
f cresc.
f cresc.
204
old, Ring the great bell at Paul's.
ff
ff
3

209
f
Two sticks and an ap - ple,
f
f
mf
213
Ring the bells at White - cha - pel.

218
Old Fa - ther Bald Pate, Ring the bells Ald - gate.
222
Maids in white a - prons,
mf

227
Ring the bells at St Cath - erine's.
232
O - ran-ges and le - mons, Ring the bells at St Cle - ment's.
f

236
f
When will you pay me?
f
f
f
241
Ring the bells at the Old Bai - ley. When I am rich, Ring the bells at Fleet-

246
- ditch.
When will that
f
251
be?
Ring the bells at Step - ney.
f

255
f cresc.
When I am old, Ring the great bell at
f cresc.
f cresc.
259
ff
Paul's.
ff
dim.
ff
ff
mf

4. *Composed upon Westminster Bridge, September 3, 1802*

William Wordsworth (1770–1850)

272
a tempo
SOPRANOS
p flessibile
ALTOS
Earth has not a - ny-thing to show more fair:
TENORS
BASSES
p flessibile
a tempo
p
mp
276
poco cresc.
Dull would he be of soul who could pass by a sight so touch-ing
poco cresc.

280
p This Ci- ty now doth like a
in its ma-jes - ty:
This Ci- ty now doth like a gar-ment wear the
p
mp
mp
284
p
beau-ty of the morn-ing;
Si - lent,
p
mp espress.
p
p

289
mp cresc.
bare, Ships, to-wers, domes, the-a-tres and tem-ples lie
mp cresc.
mp cresc.
293
f
mp dolce e dim.
o-pen un-to the fields and to the sky; All bright and glit-ter-ing
mp dolce e dim.
f
All bright and
f
mp dolce
f

297
poco rit.
a tempo
p espress.
in the smoke - less air.
Ne - ver did sun more
glit - ter - ing in the smoke - less air.
poco rit.
a tempo
mp
p espress.
mp dolce
p espress.
301
beau - ti - ful - ly steep in his first splen - dour val - ley, rock, or hill;

304
poco rit.
p dolce
Ne'er_ saw I, ne-ver felt, a calm so deep!
poco rit.
dolce
dolce
308
a tempo
poco rit.
a tempo
poco rit.
p semplice
p semplice

313
a tempo
p
The ri - ver gli-deth at his own sweet will; Dear-
p
a tempo
p
mp
317
poco rit.
a little slower
God! the ve - ry hous - es seem a - sleep; and all that migh-ty
poco rit.
a little slower
mp dolce
mp dolce

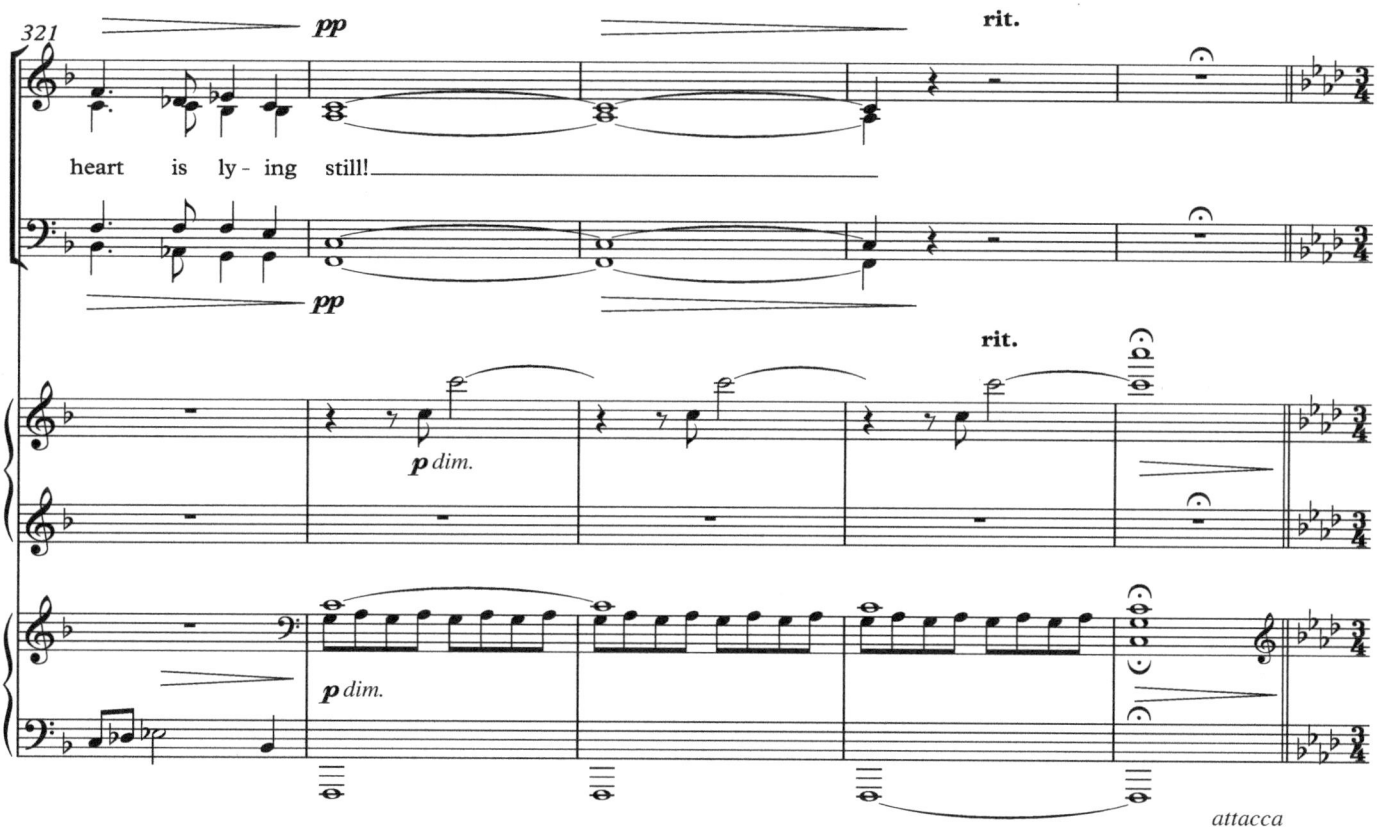

5. *Good morrow!*

Anon. (17th century, adapted)

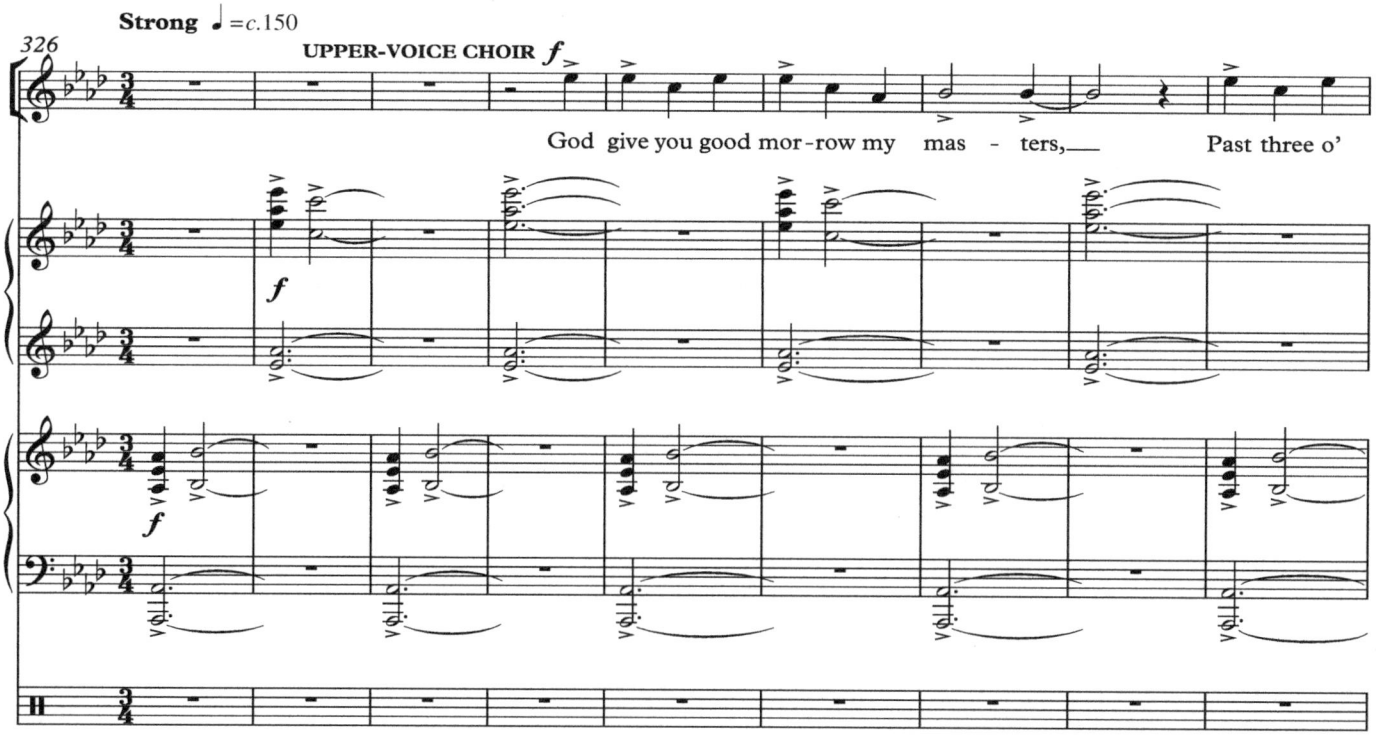

335
clock and a fair mor - ning.
p
p
TENORS & BASSES unis.
343
f
A good saus-age, a good, and it be roast - ed.

SOPRANOS & ALTOS unis.
348
f
Go round a-bout the ca - pon, go round.
f
Hot cod - lings,
cresc.
cresc.
353
New oys - ters, new!
mf
Young cab-bage
hot!
mf
White cab-bage, white,
p sub.
p sub.

357
UPPER-VOICE CHOIR
f
Broom,
ff
.&A.
white, Young par-snips, white, HEY!
ff
.&B.
White tur-nips, white, HEY!
cresc.
ff
f
cresc.
ff
f
Tambourine
tr
mf
ff
364
broom, broom!
p
p

371
SOPRANOS & ALTOS unis.
f
Will ye buy a
TENORS & BASSES unis.
f
Have you a-ny work for a tink - er?
376
mat for a bed?
New thorn-backs,
New had-dock, new!
cresc.
cresc.

382
new!
Ripe goose-ber-ries ripe,
Ripe peas-cods,
Ripe chest-nuts, ripe,
Ripe small nuts, ripe,
p sub.
cresc.
p sub.
cresc.
tr
mf
385
ff
ripe, HEY!
Sweep, chim-ney sweep,
mis - tress,
TENORS f
ff
HEY!
BASSES f
Sweep, chim - ney sweep,
ff
mf
ff
mf
ff

391
f
With a hey der-ry, der-ry, der-ry sweep.
mis - tress,
f
TENORS & BASSES unis.
From the
396
Sweep, chim - ney, sweep,
cresc.
bot - tom to the top, sweep, chim - ney sweep, Then shall no
cresc.

401
Your por - ridge pot, With a
soot fall in your por - ridge pot, With a hey der - ry, der - ry,
mf cresc.
f
mf cresc.
f
405
ff
hey der - ry, der - ry, der - ry sweep!
ff
der - ry sweep, der - ry der - ry sweep!
f

409
UPPER-VOICE CHOIR
f
Ripe straw - ber-ries, ripe!
f
416
CH.
BASSES
f
Have you a - ny
p
cresc.
p
cresc.

421
CH.
f
Cher - ry ripe, ap - ples fine, Cher - ry ripe,
S.
f
Will you buy my dish of
A.
f
Fresh cheese and cream,
T.
f
Ripe goose - ber-ries, ripe,
B.
work for a coop - er?

426
ap - ples fine,
eels?
Fine Se - ville
Hot ap - ple pies, hot, hot pip - pen pies, hot, Fine
Buy an - y ink, will you buy an - y peas?
Hard on - ions, hard,
cresc.
cresc.

430
ff
Have you
o - - ran - ges,
Young cab - bage,
le - mons, le - mons,
Young cab - bage,
Hard gar - lic, hard,
White cab - bage, white,
Ripe dam - - sons,
White cab - bage, white,

433
f
a - ny old bel - lows or trays to mend? We make an
white, Young tur - nips, white, Young par - snips, white. We make an
white, Young tur - nips, white, Young par - snips, white. We make an
White tur - nips, white, White par - snips, white. We make an
White tur - nips, white, White par - snips, white. We make an

436
ff
fff
end.
HEY!
ff
fff
end.
HEY!
ff
fff
end.
HEY!
ff
fff
end.
HEY!
ff
fff
end.
HEY!
ff
fff
ff
fff
ff
fff
ff
fff